SPEEDWEEKS
10 DAYS AT DAYTONA

SPEEDWEEKS
10 DAYS AT DAYTONA

INTRODUCTION BY DALE JARRETT

TEXT BY SANDRA MCKEE

CREATED AND PRODUCED BY MATTHEW NAYTHONS

DIRECTOR OF PHOTOGRAPHY RICK RICKMAN

EPICENTER COMMUNICATIONS

HarperEntertainment
An Imprint of HarperCollins*Publishers*

HarperCollins books may be purchased for educational, business, or sales promotional use.
For information, please write to Special Markets Department, HarperCollins Publishers Inc.,
10 East 53rd Street, New York, NY 10022.

Designed by Kelly Parisi

Printed on acid-free paper

FIRST EDITION

Library of Congress Cataloging-in-Publication Data has been applied for.

ISBN 0-06-105077-6

00 01 02 03 04 ❖ 10 9 8 7 6 5 4 3 2 1

SPEEDWEEKS

10⁴ DAYTONA

by Dale Jarrett
Three-time Daytona 500 Winner

Winning the Daytona 500 is a goal for every driver in the NASCAR Winston Cup Series. In this very competitive day and age, I don't think anyone will win seven Daytona 500s like Richard Petty did. I'm fortunate enough to have won three of them, which puts me in pretty good company with another three-time winner, Bobby Allison.

Everyone in NASCAR approaches Speedweeks and the Daytona 500 differently than any other event on our schedule. The Daytona 500 is our crown jewel, our Super Bowl, truly the Great American Race. Everyone brings the best they have to Daytona. We spend three months preparing for it. The eyes of the motorsports world are on us, not to mention the hundreds of thousands of fans who flock to Daytona for Speedweeks, and every type of media imaginable from across the nation, including live TV coverage of our races.

I didn't get much sleep the night before the February 2000 Daytona 500, and the Robert Yates Racing Quality Care Ford team got even less. We worked on our Daytona car all winter and tested it thoroughly in January. We didn't want to start the season as the defending NASCAR Winston Cup Series champions looking like we were resting on our laurels. As a driver, you want to start your engine, get rolling, and get the race underway. And you want to do it with confidence. So I'll admit I had some questions in my mind when I cranked the engine over on the afternoon of February 20.

Here's why.

Once the 500 started, I took the first three or four laps to feel the car out.

I had won the Bud Pole Award for the Daytona 500 for the second time. We used the Twin 125 to get our race setup as close to perfect as we've ever had it. But then, less than 24 hours before the race, we got into an accident during "happy hour," our final practice session. We bent the nose, a rear fender, and messed up the suspension. Our cars are very sensitive at Daytona. That's why we spend all those months tuning the chassis and getting the body as slick as we can. Our team decided to repair the car instead of going to our backup. They flew fabricators in from our shop in Charlotte. They worked on our car until 10 p.m. the night before the race, and started again at 5 a.m. on race morning.

Once the 500 started, I took the first three or four laps to feel the car out. I know how good our team is, but now I was in what was basically a rebuilt car. Could I count on it? But when I took the lead on lap 5, I knew they had made the car perfect again, and from then until lap 90, I led every lap but one. Then I hung around the top five. On lap 196, I took the lead from Johnny Benson. Two laps later the caution flag came out, and I just followed the pace car to my third Daytona 500 win.

It was an incredible job, and the credit goes to the guys who got the car back to where we had it. This was as tough a Speedweeks for our team as we've ever had. At times like this, we really find out what we're made of. I'm proud for Robert Yates, Todd Parrott, and the whole Quality Care Ford team, because this Daytona 500 win belongs to them.

This book really captures the spirit, competition, excitement, and fun of Speedweeks. The team of photographers did a precision job, just like the folks who worked on our car. I think they got it perfect—and I hope you enjoy the result.

In a sport that thrives on family and tradition, Richard Petty is "The King" in more than one sense. Decked out here in his plumbed cowboy hat and boots, he prowls the garage as an owner, keeping tabs on the race cars of his son Kyle, and John Andretti. But Richard knows every inch of Daytona International Speedway as a driver, too. He is the sport's first seven-time champion. Before television broadcasts, Petty built a fan base one handshake and one autograph at a time. His signature is a work of art.

Car owner Joe Gibbs is famous for coaching the Washington Redskins to three Super Bowl victories. But while he was making the NFL franchise one of the most successful in the business, his eyes kept straying to racing. As a kid, he wanted to grow up to be Richard Petty. Now he's chasing a cherished first NASCAR Winston Cup title with his drivers Bobby Labonte and Tony Stewart and getting help in the quest from his two sons, Cory and J.D., who work on the team.

Darrell Waltrip, 53, was the original "Jaws," the college-educated whippersnapper who came to NASCAR Winston Cup racing in the 1970s and thought he knew as much as "The Good ol' Boys." He laid the groundwork for drivers such as Jeff Gordon and Tony Stewart and won three championships by 1985. But it took him 17 years to win his first Daytona 500 in 1989. When he did, he put on one of the best remembered victory dances ever witnessed in Daytona's storied winner's circle. Daytona 2000 was his final 500. He will step to the sidelines at the end of this season and join Fox in the broadcast booth.

Flamboyant and handsome Felix Sabates symbolizes NASCAR and the American Dream. A Cuban-born American, he is a self-made man. He began by creating Top Sales Co., which represents manufacturers of electronic, computer and related businesses, added American Showboats and builds mega-yachts over 100 feet. Sabates now enjoys the benefits of all the labor. Corporate jets. Private planes. Mega-yachts. And a two-car stable of NASCAR Winston Cup Series race teams.

Moguls in the wings. Above, International Speedway Corporation's Bill France (left) and New York captain of industry Donald Trump meet at Daytona International Speedway. France is the man who took over from his father, NASCAR founder Bill France Sr., and charted the course to the sport's success. He saw the future, visualizing big sponsorships and advertising and superstars. In Trump, France has found an equally forward-thinking businessman. But where France is basically thoughtful and measured, Trump is brash and bold. Together, they are working on an effort to bring a major speedway to the greater New York area.

At right, Jackie Joyner-Kersee has made her way from the slums of East St. Louis to become an Olympic track and field legend. Like many in NASCAR, she, too, is known for her good works and brings a bright spirit to NASCAR Winston Cup racing. At Daytona, where she served as grand marshal, she and her husband, Bob, familiarized themselves with the scene as they continue working to find sponsorship for their own team.

Traditions are found in many places in Daytona. At right, the drivers' meeting, a gathering of drivers, crew chiefs, owners and NASCAR officials that precedes every race. Among those assembled here are drivers Jeff Gordon, Sterling Marlin and Bobby Labonte, crew chief Tony Glover, International Speedway Corp executive vice president Lesa Kennedy and NASCAR senior vice president Brian France. The meeting is called to order and a roll call taken. A dissertation on the rules of the road: pit road speed limits, patience, courtesy and safety follows. It is also here that drivers are told about any special circumstance that might impact the day's race such as weather conditions or tire wear. And it is here that drivers have their last opportunity to voice any concerns before the race.

Looking at the photo to the left, the temptation is to say, "Big Man in town!" and you wouldn't be wrong. As a child, Dale Jarrett played in the infield he now observes. But these days he is the reigning NASCAR Winston Cup champion. And, like his dad, Ned, who won two NASCAR Winston Cup titles, Dale brings more to his sport than pure racing skill. He also exudes patience, grace and warmth.

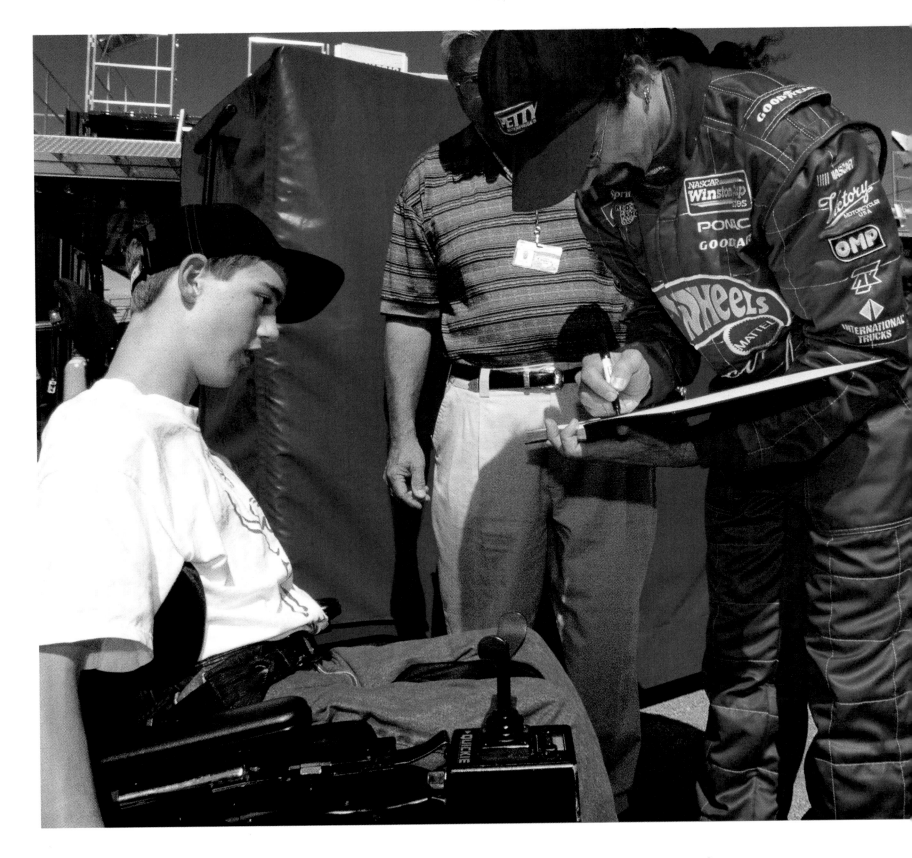

Make a wish, and you get Kyle Petty (above). He is the son of Richard Petty and the grandson of the late Lee Petty, NASCAR's first Daytona 500 winner in 1959. But while Kyle has raced, it is his work off the track that has made him a star. "If you only look at the racing, he didn't do what I did," said his father, Richard, who has 200 victories. "But if you look at what else he's accomplished — his charity work, his family, the NASCAR Man of the Year award — he's got the biggest heart in the sport and he's accomplished things I haven't. I'm super,

super proud of Kyle." Each year Kyle raises money for the Racing Wives Auxiliary and children's hospitals with the Kyle Petty Charity Ride Across America. And, like his father, he never seems too busy to sign an autograph or bring a little happiness to a child.

Tony Stewart (above) has hit NASCAR Winston Cup racing like a tornado from his home state of Indiana. A year ago, he and his team set rookie records by winning three races and finishing fourth in the NASCAR Winston Cup points race. Now, Stewart faces a bevy of microphones and media questions daily, as he is considered a contender for the Daytona 500 and the NASCAR Winston Cup title.

At right, chef Scott Lato of Tallahassee, Fla., is caught as he is about to start preparing shrimp gumbo for the corporate crowd in the suites high above the track's start-finish line.

NASCAR Busch Series driver Ron Hornaday (above) looks concerned as he waits for the NAPA Auto Parts 300. The 300 runs Saturday, the day before the Daytona 500 and kicks off the season for the NASCAR Busch Series drivers. It sets the stage for the entire season — just as Sunday's 500 does for the Winston Cup drivers. Hornaday, who started on the outside of the front row, led 42 of the first 62 laps before getting involved in a crash and finishing 32nd.

Meanwhile, NASCAR Winston Cup car owner Jack Roush (right) is cool as he checks lap times on the team's computer. Roush is a Ford man. You look at him and think Ford. Think

basic. Think reliable. Roush and his teams perform consistently year after year. A businessman, he believes bigger can be better and fields six teams to prove it. His competition can't quite grasp it. But Roush, his basic production plan in place, goes on and on, like a Ford assembly line.

On the following page, meet Lois Tyler, 69, who is celebrating a 40th anniversary. She's posing with a 1961 amphibian car from Germany, but her real claim to fame is that she is one of just seven women to race the high banks of Daytona. She did it in 1960 in the Women's National Championship Race, a two-lap special.

Women's Natl–Championship Rac

Nascar Legend Driver

Lois Tyler–Daytona

January 31, 1960–#69

NASCAR 2000

With early morning comes the beginning of long days at Daytona International Speedway — for everyone. Preparing for a week of racing, that takes in everything from NASCAR's Craftsman Truck Series to its NASCAR Busch and NASCAR Winston Cup Series, demands determined, concentrated efforts. Whether it is the fans arriving early for a day of racing or crewmen setting up the cars, as on the previous pages, or waiting patiently in line to get on the track to qualify — as Chad Little's John Deere team is doing at right — everyone has a job to do.

Goodyear tires are what keep the cars and drivers attached to the racetrack. The placement of the tire on the right or left rear or front will determine its air pressure. Throughout a day of practice or racing tire technicians check those pressures and measure the heat after every stop. At right, NASCAR Winston Cup driver Rusty Wallace gets ready for a lap of IROC (International Race of Champions) practice. IROC is a series of four races designed to produce a winner based solely on driver skill. Twelve drivers who have won major races or major championships are invited to compete in equally prepared Firebirds. The series begins at Daytona and then makes three more stops at tracks chosen for their diversity over the next six months.

Adam Petty, above, ran in his second NASCAR Busch Series season in preparation for a NASCAR Winston Cup debut. At Daytona, young Adam's eyes show his strong-willed determination. Adam is the fourth generation of Pettys to race at Daytona, following great-grandfather Lee, grandfather Richard, and father Kyle. At right, Kyle checks a tire that has just come off his son's car.

Crewman Jonathan Davis checks the temperature on a tire that has just come off Mark Martin's Valvoline Ford during practice. The idea is to read the measurements and determine the tire pressures the car will need for the race. NASCAR Winston Cup teams have what seem to be a million small gadgets they use for measurements, communications and assorted other chores — like making the car run. Below, all hands are at work on a carburetor.

Ricky Rudd's team will shine on pit road after crewman Tracy Lumpkin delivers the team's freshly dry-cleaned uniforms. If this was baseball, Lumpkin would be known as the "Utility Infielder," the guy who can play any position and get the job done. Lumpkin drives the team's big rig, but he also doubles as a handyman, who does the team laundry and makes runs to the dry cleaners.

Below, a crew member gets a reading on Kyle Petty's lap times — or a competitor's. Teams keep track of their own times, as well as those of others, to measure how much of an advantage they may have or how much more work they still need to do.

NASCAR Winston Cup car owner Richard Childress may not have been the first to come up with a check list for his team to follow on race day morning, but he was one of the first to put it in writing. On the following page, you can see it taped to Dale Earnhardt's Goodwrench Chevrolet prior to the 500.

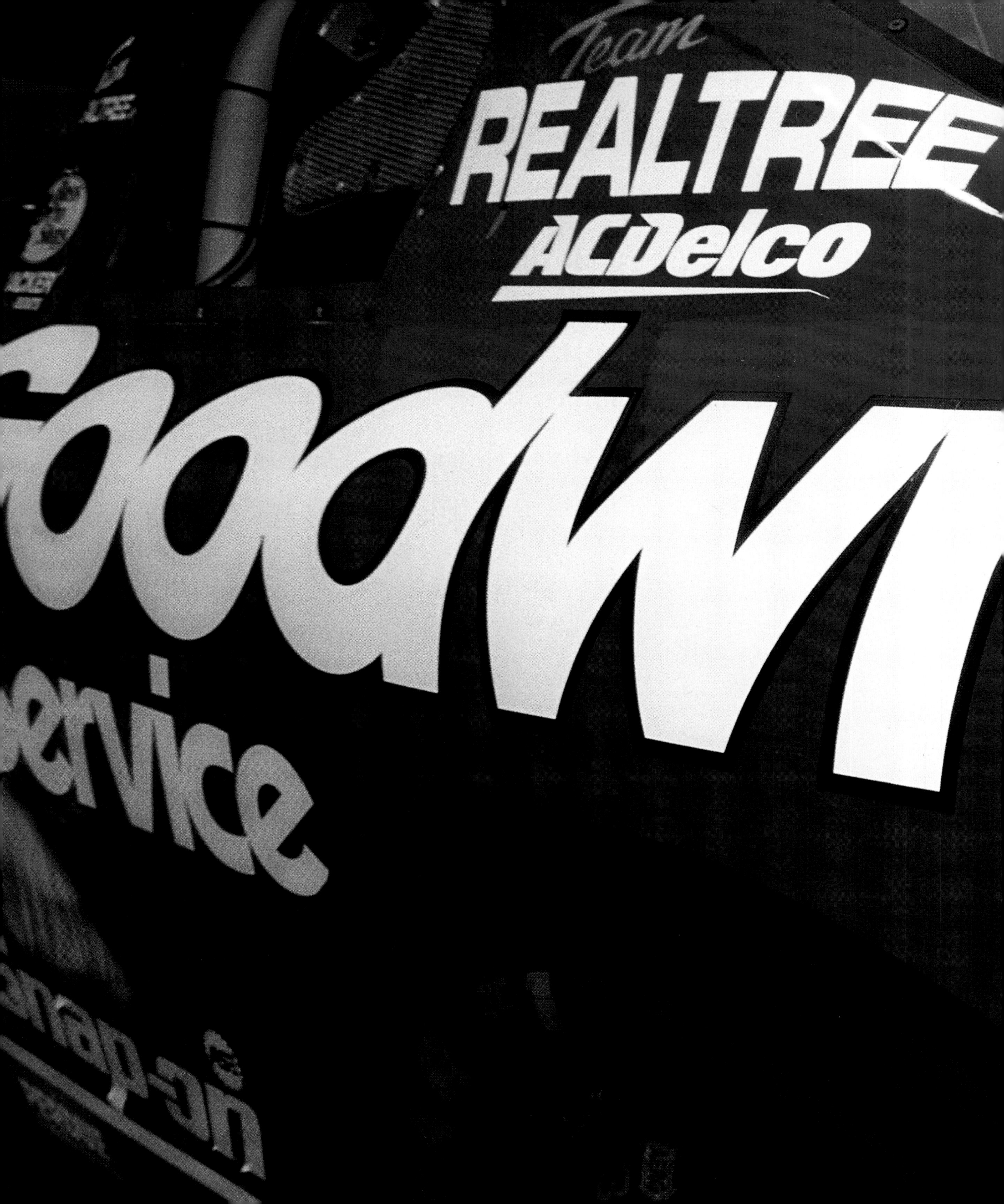
Team
REALTREE
ACDelco
service

RCR RACEDAY CHECKLIST CON'T

___ **MISC.:** (Mike Moore)

___ EMPTY WATER OVERFLOW TANK IN TRUNK
___ CHECK CHAINS FRONT & REAR
___ CHECK JACK STOPS FOR HEIGHT & CLEARANCE (WITH LOW RACE AIR)
___ MARK JACK STOPS

DANNY LAWRENCE / JERRY HAILEY:

___ **ENGINE**

___ ADJUST VALVES / TORQUE ADJUSTING NUTS & BOLTS
___ SEAL VALVE COVERS
___ CHECK O'BERG
___ CHECK CLUTCH Z BAR & ADJUSTING NUTS
___ COVER ON OIL FILTER
___ CERAMIC SEAL IN RADIATOR
___ CHECK WATER & OIL LEVELS
___ TOP & BOTTOM RADIATOR HOSES TIGHT
___ OVERFLOW HOSE & SURGE TANK BLEEDER LINE TIGHT
___ CORRECT FAN BLADE & BOLTS TIGHT **OR** CHECK ELECTRIC FAN FOR WORKING PROPE
___ CHECK FUEL PUMP BOLTS
___ CHECK BELT TENSIONS & CONDITION
___ CHECK ALL LINES FOR TIGHTNESS & LEAKS
___ CHECK OIL PAN & FRONT COVER FOR LEAKS
___ CHECK ALL OIL LINES FOR HEADER CLEARANCE
___ CHECK STARTER WIRE FOR HEADER CLEARANCE
___ INTAKE MANIFOLD BOLTS TIGHT
___ CARB BOWLS SECURED & JETS CORRECT SIZE
___ CHECK DISTRIBUTOR CAP & TIE-DOWN WIRES
___ CHECK ALTERNAOR FOR TIGHTNESS, WIRES & SEE IF CHARGING PROPERLY
___ SECURE / TAPE ALTERNATOR WIRE CONNECTION
___ CHECK HEADER BOLTS
___ MAKE SURE VALVE COVER BOLTS ARE 3MD
___ CHECK THROTTLE RETURN SPRINGS
___ PUT IN RACE SPARK PLUGS, DOUBLE CHECK WIRES, SILICONE TO HEADS
___ CHECK GAS LINES (TIGHTNESS & LEAKS)
___ LUBRICATE THROTTLE HEIMS & CHECK FOR WIDE OPEN
___ CHECK STARTER BOLTS
___ CHECK CARB. TIGHT
___ CHECK IDLE SPEED
___ CHECK DRAIN PLUGS IN BLOCK
___ CHECK AIR CLEANER ASS. & ELEMENT, THOROUGHLY SEALED TO COWL AIR BOX
___ CHECK ALL MISC. BOLTS
___ INSTALL GUARD ON OIL PUMP BELT
___ DOUBLE CHECK SPARK PLUG WIRES & TIE & SECURE!
___ HEAT SHIELDS SECURED
___ RUBBER SEALING WASHER FOR AIR CLEANER ASS.
___ CHECK VALVE SPRING COOLER
___ CHECK SHIFT LIGHT / REV LIMITER CHIP
___ CHECK TIMING
___ PREPARE SPARE CARB.
___ CHECK QUICK - FILL ON RADIATOR
___ HOSE INSTALLED FOR FUEL TUBE TO AIR CLEANER TOP

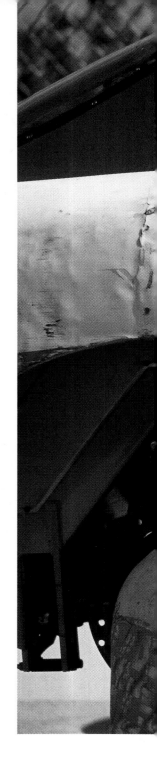

It's fuel to go at left, as a crewman for the John Andretti team hauls gas from the NASCAR-sanctioned pump to the pits for the race. All the teams use the same Tosco 76 fuel supply and they fetch it in these 11-gallon cans. During a normal pit stop, a crew will put two full cans into the car's gas tank. Crew chief Gil Martin, left above, directs Amoco crewman Shane Westerberg as the team works feverishly to repaint the car after its original sheet metal was torn up when rookie Dave Blaney accidentally brushed the wall during practice prior to the Daytona 500.

After a practice session, teammates Rusty Wallace (far left) and Jeremy Mayfield confer. Drivers and crew chiefs have hundreds of discussions during the weeks leading up to the race. On teams with more than one car competing, drivers may also discuss their race cars with their teammates. A year ago, Rusty Wallace and Jeremy Mayfield decided that while they were working for the same owner, the information flow between the two of them would be limited. Each tried to set up his car in a way that best suited himself. This season, however, it isn't unusual to see the two of them, as they are at left, in deep discussions. Going into Daytona, the two had promised to work hand-in-hand to make both their cars more similar in an effort to make them both run better.

Below, defending NASCAR Winston Cup champion Dale Jarrett finds it a regular part of the program to meet the press at the end of a day's practice.

Seven-time NASCAR Winston Cup champion Dale Earnhardt, in car at right, came into Daytona 2000 saying "I think I have to be the man to beat." He said it because of his consistently high finishes in the 500 and because he has won a record 34 times in various events at the speedway. But by the time the 500 was ready to start, Earnhardt had a headache from all the difficulty he and his team were having trying to make his Chevrolet run fast under NASCAR's new shock and spring rules. For the first time in 10 straight years Earnhardt didn't win one of the Twin 125-mile qualifying races. And when the 500 was over, he was a disappointing 21st.

Taking no chances, crewmen for Rusty Wallace's team, above, are in the midst of an engine change on Wallace's Ford prior to lining up the car for the start of the big race. At right, two NASCAR Busch Series officials Pete Babb and Lou Williams patrol pit road prior to and during the race monitoring pit stops, making sure tires are collected, making sure speed limits are observed. If a violation occurs, the officials can have a car brought back to the pits for a stop-and-go penalty.

By the end of two weeks' work, Rusty Wallace's Miller Lite Ford sat ready and waiting for the start of the Daytona 500. Searching for his 50th NASCAR Winston Cup victory and his first in the Daytona 500, Wallace had great hopes. But, despite a great run, he was forced to settle for a fourth-place finish.

Though the work is all-consuming, time can be found to share heartfelt moments like a prayer with Adam Petty on the preceding page; Rusty Wallace's motorcycle ride with his wife, Patti, left; and Dale Earnhardt's heart-to-heart with driver Steve Park, who drives the Earnhardt-owned Pennzoil car. Earnhardt also fields a NASCAR Winston Cup car for his son Dale Earnhardt Jr. in this family-dominated sport.

In one of the most amazing transformations in sports, NASCAR Winston Cup racing has traveled the North Carolina back roads to Main Street, USA. Along the way, it has become one of the most family-dominated of professional sports. You can find families throughout the grandstands and infields, in the garage, in the NASCAR executive offices and in the drivers' family areas at the tracks. There are fathers and sons, fathers and daughters, grandfathers and grandsons and brothers in residence. At left, Jeff Burton and his 4-year-old daughter, Paige, enjoys some play time at the playground in the drivers' area at the race track. The playground is part of what creates "a community" at the track for the children, as well as the parents.

Above, three-time NASCAR Winston Cup champion Jeff Gordon enjoys a sunny stroll with his wife, Brooke. Brooke says all she ever wanted was "to marry someone who truly loved me." And Jeff seldom misses the opportunity to say publicly just how much he does love her. Despite all the traveling his job demands, they have spent only three nights apart in their nearly six years of marriage.

Katie McLaughlin leaves pit road, where her husband, NASCAR Busch driver Mike McLaughlin, has just finished qualifying on the outside of the front row for the NAPA 300. Katie was due to deliver at any moment. But she wanted to be at the track with her husband and, being a veteran mom (Katie has delivered two other children), she felt comfortable being at the track. Still, she had also made arrangements for an obstetrician to meet her at Halifax Medical Center, or to have the baby at the speedway in the infield care center if necessary. Katie made it through race week and gave birth to Michael Thomas, called Max by the proud parents, on Leap Day, Feb. 29.

At left, Chase Elliott, 4, keeps in touch with his dad, Bill, the 1988 NASCAR Winston Cup champion and two-time Daytona 500 winner, via a headset from the pits. Further along pit road, Adam Petty, above, gets a few words of advice from his dad, Kyle.

On Sunday mornings before every race drivers, crew chiefs and team owners assemble for the pre-race drivers' meeting and then end the assembly with a prayer. At Daytona, it is no different. Among those with bowed heads below are Jeff Gordon, far right, with his car owner Rick Hendrick beside him. Both men have much to be thankful for. These Daytona Speedweeks were the first for Hendrick, 50, in three years, as he fought to recover from leukemia. And this Sunday morning drivers' meeting was the first he had shared with members of his team and the NASCAR family since November 1996. "I'm grateful for a second chance," Hendrick said, reflecting on the cancer being in remission. "I don't want to be too sentimental, but I never thought I'd feel this good again."

From the hands of one generation to the next generation and to the next, that's how the Frances have built the family business. First there was Bill France, who founded NASCAR and set the sport of stock car racing on its way. Then came Bill Jr., who succeeded his father as president, and saw the future before anyone else. He envisioned national recognition, major sponsorships and superstars. Now his children, Brian, seen here, and his sister Lesa France Kennedy, are carrying on the tradition. Brian is senior vice president of NASCAR, directing all aspects of marketing, while Lesa is executive vice president of International Speedway Corp., which owns and operates motorsports facilities around the country.

God and country are always part of the NASCAR Speedweeks scene. Here Jeff Burton has a private prayer with Motor Racing Outreach founder Max Helton. Billy Wilbern, right, the front tire changer on the Miller Lite Ford, demonstrates his loyalty as the national anthem is sung.

A lot of smiles were in evidence before the 42nd annual Daytona 500. Jeff Burton and his wife, Kim, were obviously in a good mood as they headed toward pit road for the start of the race.

Families, of course, come in all forms in NASCAR. While drivers will do almost anything to win on the race track, they are some of the best companions on the sidelines. They park side-by-side in the drivers' parking area, go to church together and some even vacation together. At left, Dale Jarrett, Rusty Wallace, Scott Pruett and Bill Elliott listen to Mark Martin as he shares a "fishing story" while they wait for the start of Thursday's Twin 125-mile qualifying race.

Terry and Bobby Labonte are just one of five sets of brothers who compete on the NASCAR Winston Cup trail. While they are close friends off the track, going so far as to park their motor homes next to each other in the drivers' park, it is a different story when they go to work. Terry, who drives the No. 5 Kellogg's Chevrolet for Rick Hendrick, and Bobby, who motors along in the No. 18 Interstate Batteries Pontiac for Joe Gibbs, love nothing better than to rub a little sheet metal and beat each other to the finish line. Terry has two NASCAR Winston Cup titles, while Bobby is trying to win his first. Above, fans display their creative loyalties.

Fathers can't seem to wait to get their children involved in NASCAR Winston Cup racing, the sport they love. As demonstrated here, fathers and sons of all ages come to the races.

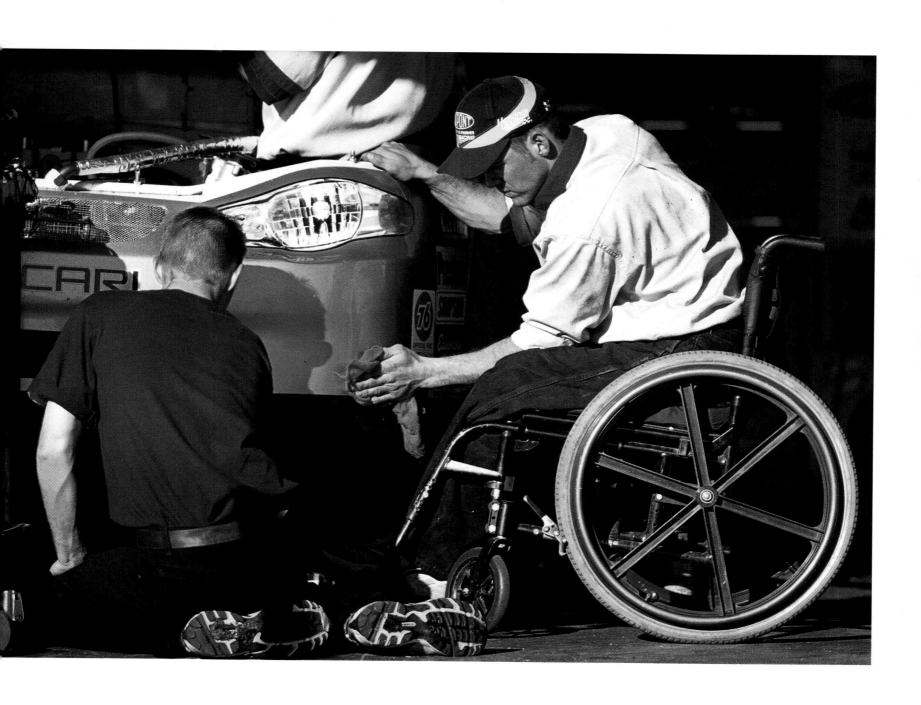

As the third generation of the France family becomes more and more prominent within the organization, they are also becoming more and more visible around the racetrack. Lesa France Kennedy was spotted in the garage area, at the drivers' meeting and here, outside of Daytona USA, during Speedweeks. Lesa, executive vice president of ISC, is one of the driving forces behind the new racetracks in Kansas City and the Chicago area that will open next season.

Weddings, nearly 20 of them, were held at The Speedway during Speedweeks. But when Palmyra, N.J., residents Margaret and Tom Fee, above, said "I do" on Wednesday of race week, their vows were witnessed by NASCAR Winston Cup driver Michael Waltrip. Margaret had called her favorite driver eight months in advance to ask if he would be one of their witnesses. It was the first time Waltrip had been party to a fan's wedding. In fact, it was the first time any driver had taken part in such a ceremony at the track, officials said.

From the waving of the green flag by Jackie Joyner-Kersee (preceding page) to start the NASCAR Winston Cup Series to the closing laps, drivers have to be constantly on alert for disaster — spilled oil, a piece of debris, a low flying bird or a spinning race car suddenly appearing before them. Whether it is in the Busch race, the Daytona 500 or any other event during Speedweeks, every driver in the field has to follow the pace car for the start and for every restart thereafter. It's a tricky business. With lapped cars on the low side and the leaders on the high side, everyone is busy staking out their positions. Drivers warm their tires by weaving their cars back and forth. In the middle of the pack and farther back, drivers are hoping to get through the first green flag lap at the start and on the restarts without getting caught in an accident that could be created by the overzealous. Some drivers will drop back a little, hoping for a running start that will build their cars' momentum and at the same time allow them to see openings in the traffic ahead.

The driver at the front of the field on the low side is hoping the car behind him is strong enough to team with him to get a strong, fast start. Together, perhaps, they can get by the race leader to regain a lap they have already lost. Beside him, the leader is making plans to use the start for his own advantage. As drivers become more and more experienced, their game plans become more sophisticated. In past 500s, Jeff Gordon has brought the field down so slowly it has appeared the cars would stall before they ever got going. And Rusty Wallace has been accused of "jumping" the start, putting his foot on the gas pedal long before the green flag flies and long before the start/finish line. But the idea is to do what's best for your own car. The race leader is the man in charge — everyone else simply has to tough it out.

The work on the sidelines is every bit as swift as that on the track. During a regular pit stop under the green flag, crews move at lightning speed to change four tires, wash the windshield, fill the car with gas, make a chassis adjustment and give their drivers a drink. It's all accomplished in about 15 or 16 seconds flat.

While the NASCAR Winston Cup cars zoom around the track so fast they often seem a blur, a group of individuals, as seen on the following page, called "spotters," are watching with eagle-like eyes. Spotters are responsible for their individual drivers' safety. At Daytona, where speeds soar toward 200 mph, it can be a mentally draining task. The spotter watches for slow cars, for accidents, for clearance during a pass involving his driver. What he sees, he relays to the man behind the wheel through the team radio. "Just think about it," said Don Cox, one of Jeff Gordon's two spotters at the 500. "We have the driver's life in our hands every minute of the race."

The tire change at Daytona has to be a work of art. On the preceding page, Lowe's crewman Sean Irvan, carrying the tire, follows front tire changer Greg Burkhart onto pit road to begin a four-tire change. In massive congestion, with other race cars roaring past, they must be totally focused on their jobs. Anything left undone can be the difference between an incident-free race and a mishap and between winning and losing.

At right, the congestion during Saturday's Goody's 300 NASCAR Busch Series race can be seen as tire carrier Dave Goulet also acts as traffic cop for Jay Sauter in the Quality Farm and Country Chevrolet. Sauter finished fourth.

NASCAR Winston Cup cars may look simple enough, but a lot of high-tech work goes on behind the scenes to make them capable of doing what they do. At left, Tony Stewart's shock specialist Ronnie Crooks and crew chief Greg Zipadelli, behind him, confer over computer printouts on "the pit box," a metal cabinet that includes everything from built-in director's chairs to video display equipment to computer data bases. The best of the best compete in the International Race of Champions, a series of four races in identically prepared Pontiac Firebirds. Below, NASCAR Winston Cup champion Dale Jarrett is being told to "hurry up!" by Indy Racing League champion Greg Ray. Dale Earnhardt, who won the IROC title last year, is riding along at the top of the track. He eventually found his way to the front for his sixth IROC victory at Daytona. Overall, it was Earnhardt's 34th career win at the famous tri-oval.

Robin Pemberton knows he has spotters around Daytona's 2.5 mile tri-oval, but that doesn't mean another set of eyes won't help his driver, Rusty Wallace, get closer to victory lane. Pemberton, a 16-year veteran and the man in charge of Wallace's team for the last six years, is keeping lookout, while gas man Bob Tracey also keeps his eyes on the racetrack.

The Interstate Batteries team demonstrates the hustle and muscle necessary for a good pit stop, as two of its members give Bobby Labonte a can of fuel. Meanwhile, Dale Earnhardt's GM Goodwrench team demonstrates what a team does between the frantic pit ballet, as it sits and watches for its Chevrolet. The view from the pit is one of the most limited. Crews can see only from the fourth turn down the front stretch to Turn 1. Most other information comes to them via their headsets.

During the NASCAR Busch Series race, tire carrier Terry Hearn appears to have a bird's-eye view as he keeps watch for his driver Elton Sawyer. Sawyer eventually finished 30th.

On Saturday afternoon, Ron Hornaday, in car No. 3 below, is running ahead of this pack of drivers that includes Tony Raines (33), Michael Waltrip (7) and Chad Chaffin (77).

Two days before the 500, NASCAR's Craftsman Truck Series, on the following page, put on a thrilling, high-speed show. It was the first race at Daytona since 1988 without restrictor plates, which are used to limit the air flow to the engine and thus reduce speeds. The trucks made old-fashioned slingshot passes that had the Daytona fans on the edges of their seats most of Friday afternoon.

Following page: During the NASCAR Busch Series race, it seemed everyone was on the lookout on pit road and from inside tents in the infield.

Friday afternoon, just days before the Daytona 500, NASCAR Winston Cup driver Geoffrey Bodine, in truck No. 15, goes for a crazy ride during the NASCAR Craftsman Truck Series debut at Daytona International Speedway. On lap 57, Bodine is caught in what looks like the worst accident in the Speedway's history. His truck takes flight, hits the retaining wall and erupts into flames. A total of 13 trucks go spinning, prompting driver Jimmy Hensley to say, "It was like being inside a pinball machine." For Bodine, it was worse, but after a dizzying ride, he was the perfect example of the perfect driver, exhibiting durability, fearlessness, tenacity and daring. Bodine had all the right stuff, as metal scraped against concrete and flames blew past him. "I just went for a wild ride," he said later and no one disagreed.

CBS, which began broadcasting the Daytona 500 in 1979, has seen many changes over the past 22 years. Here, personnel in the control booth for the network's final 500 broadcast watch numerous screens before quickly deciding which images make the broadcast. In 2001, Fox Television will take over the broadcast of the Daytona 500 and the first half of the NASCAR Winston Cup Series schedule.

At Daytona, fans go in search of drivers, like Robby
Gordon, seen above in a moment of relaxation in his
motor home, and they go in search of fun. Sometimes,
as on the preceding page, they enjoy a night at Razzles
Disco. At other times, however, some are just as happy
with a solitary moment at The Cruisin Cafe, where
autographed photos and memorabilia leave little doubt
Richard Petty is still The King.

Some visitors to Daytona Beach enjoy a last, historic drive on the white sands near the center of town. Officials planned to bar cars from the busiest part of town shortly after Speedweeks. At right, fans also relax at the Ocean Deck, a popular beach bar that offers reggae music inside and the sandy beach, complete with volleyball court, just one step off its deck.

Car owner Felix Sabates, above left, is host to a pre-race party on his yacht, the *Monte Carlo*. With him are NASCAR Winston Cup driver Sterling Marlin and his wife, Paula. At the same gathering, Emilie Petrocelli and Sarah Gurtis, center, enjoy camaraderie around the buffet. The yacht, like that of a number of other NASCAR Winston Cup car owners and drivers, is docked in the Halifax Harbor Marina, where the peaceful mornings and evenings are in high contrast to the frenetic, high-speed pace at the Speedway.

NASCAR Winston Cup fans may come for a weekend or the entire week. They come in RVs, campers and motor homes, and some simply drive down in the family car or truck and pitch a tent. They set up camp. Move in. It's Home Sweet Home, as they enjoy the warm sunshine, the view and each other.

It's lunch time! And that means different things to different teams. For a number of big teams, like Roush Racing, it can mean a walk over to the team's hospitality tent near victory lane. That's what crew chief Frank Stoddard, his driver Jeff Burton, their Exide crew and a few members of Mark Martin's Valvoline crew have done, above.

For others, like Bobby Hillin Jr.'s NASCAR Busch Grand National Kleenex team, lunch simply can be a cookout prepared by a crew member who doubles as cook. At right, Bud Howland, whose main job is to drive the team's tractor-trailer from race to race, relishes his work at the grill.

Chad Little and Jeff Burton, teammates on the Jack Roush-owned teams, exchange stories under the February sun, above, while at right, Jason Poole soaks up a quiet moment before the 500. During the race, Poole is the "catch-can man" for Rusty Wallace. That means he is responsible for collecting any fuel that overflows during the team's pit stops.

Exide crewman Pierre Kuettel had his hands full at Daytona. NASCAR imposed new shock absorber rules and Kuettel is the Exide team's shocks specialist. Here he takes a moment to review his data.

Throughout Speedweeks, children can be found almost everywhere playing with race cars or trading cards and dreaming of their NASCAR Winston Cup heroes. Those below have their imagination captured by a "build your own race car" exhibit at The Home Depot. On the following page, Jeff Burton, reading the *USA Today* sports section, and his team make the most of a midweek break in the action to chill out in the team's transporter.

For an entire week "The Sultan of Sand" worked on the construction of this sand castle that was completed on the day of the 500. The artwork greeted the nearly 3,000 VIP members of the Daytona Club each time they came to the facility located behind the Winston Tower.

Fans, like those above, delight in the Daytona Club's variety of video games that offered skeet shooting in an Everglade theme area, hang gliding in the Key West area, jet skiing in South Beach and racing games in Daytona Beach. The huge quadrangle-designed tent presentation also coordinated its food service with the theme designs.

On the following pages, fans jam the souvenir row, make use of the infield drugstore and settle down for a family evening around a campfire.

NASCAR Winston Cup rookie Matt Kenseth, above, enjoys his first victory at Daytona International Speedway. But the win came in the NASCAR Busch Series' NAPA Auto Parts 300. At right, Ricky Rudd, another first-time winner at Daytona, receives high-fives from his crew as he comes down pit road after winning the second of Thursday's Gatorade Twin 125-Mile Qualifying races. The Twins determine starting spots three-through-43 for the 500. The first two starting spots are determined during pole day qualifying the previous Saturday. If, as in this, one or both of the Twin 125 race winners has already secured a front row starting spot, the second place finisher gets the second row spot and everyone else moves up a position behind him. In this case, Rudd had already secured his seat on the outside of the front row, thus Mike Skinner, who finished second to Rudd in the Twin 125 race, earned the outside spot on the second row.

Celebrations take all forms around the speedway, as both the sport's fans and participants demonstrate their emotions. Fans jump for joy and the Ford Quality Care team of Dale Jarrett shares a moment of satisfaction when Jarrett comes home the Daytona 500 winner.

Mike Wallace, above, pumps his fist with delight as he celebrates being the first driver ever to win a NASCAR Craftsman Truck Series race at Daytona International Speedway. The thrilling Friday afternoon race was the first for the series at the 2.5-mile track. It wasn't Bill Elliott's first trip to Daytona's victory lane, at right, but it might have felt like it. Though Elliott, a two-time Daytona 500 winner, dominated superspeedway racing prior to the coming of restrictor plates, it had been eight years since he had visited victory lane during Speedweeks.

When Dale Jarrett was a little boy, he dreamed about winning the Daytona 500 — just once. But here, on a glorious day at the start of a new century, Jarrett (right) and the owner of his Quality Care Ford, Robert Yates (above), find themselves jubilantly celebrating Jarrett's third victory in the 52-year-old classic. "It's really incredible," said Jarrett, 43, who also won the 500 in 1993 and 1996. "It sends chills down my spine." As well it might. Jarrett is the son of two-time NASCAR Winston Cup champion Ned Jarrett. But Ned never won the Daytona 500. Now, Dale is in the company of the legendary Bobby Allison, tied for third on the Daytona 500's all-time victory list. Only Richard Petty, with seven 500 victories, and Cale Yarborough, with four, have more.

Trophies are everywhere you look in Daytona's victory lane. Robert Yates glows as he holds the Governor's Cup on the preceding page. Above, the incredible Harley J. Earl Daytona 500 Trophy that goes to the winning driver is a detailed study of an experimental concept car designed by Earl in the early 1950s. Jarrett's crew chief Todd Parrott, not pictured, also received the Cannonball Baker Award. The Daytona 500 is the only race in which the driver, owner and crew chief each receive a special piece of hardware.

Right, Florida 200 winner Robert Huffman celebrates after parking his No. 37 White House Apple Juice Pontiac in the winner's circle. The Florida 200 is part of the Goody's Dash Series, a touring division for compact cars in NASCAR. The Goody's Dash race is one of eight support races in six different series that are run over nine days leading up to the Daytona 500. And it is all those races that put the true meaning in Speedweeks at Daytona International Speedway.

On the following pages, next: Daytona 500 winner Dale Jarrett waves to the fans as he takes his victory lap. Jarrett became only the fourth driver in history to win the 500 three or more times. Next, Crewmen for John Andretti load his car into the team's hauler. Andretti, who drives Richard Petty's famous No. 43, started 30th in the 500 and finished 22nd. On race day, even before the morning fog has burned off the race track, workers are busy putting a shine on seats for the 500, which is always sold out a year — or more — in advance.

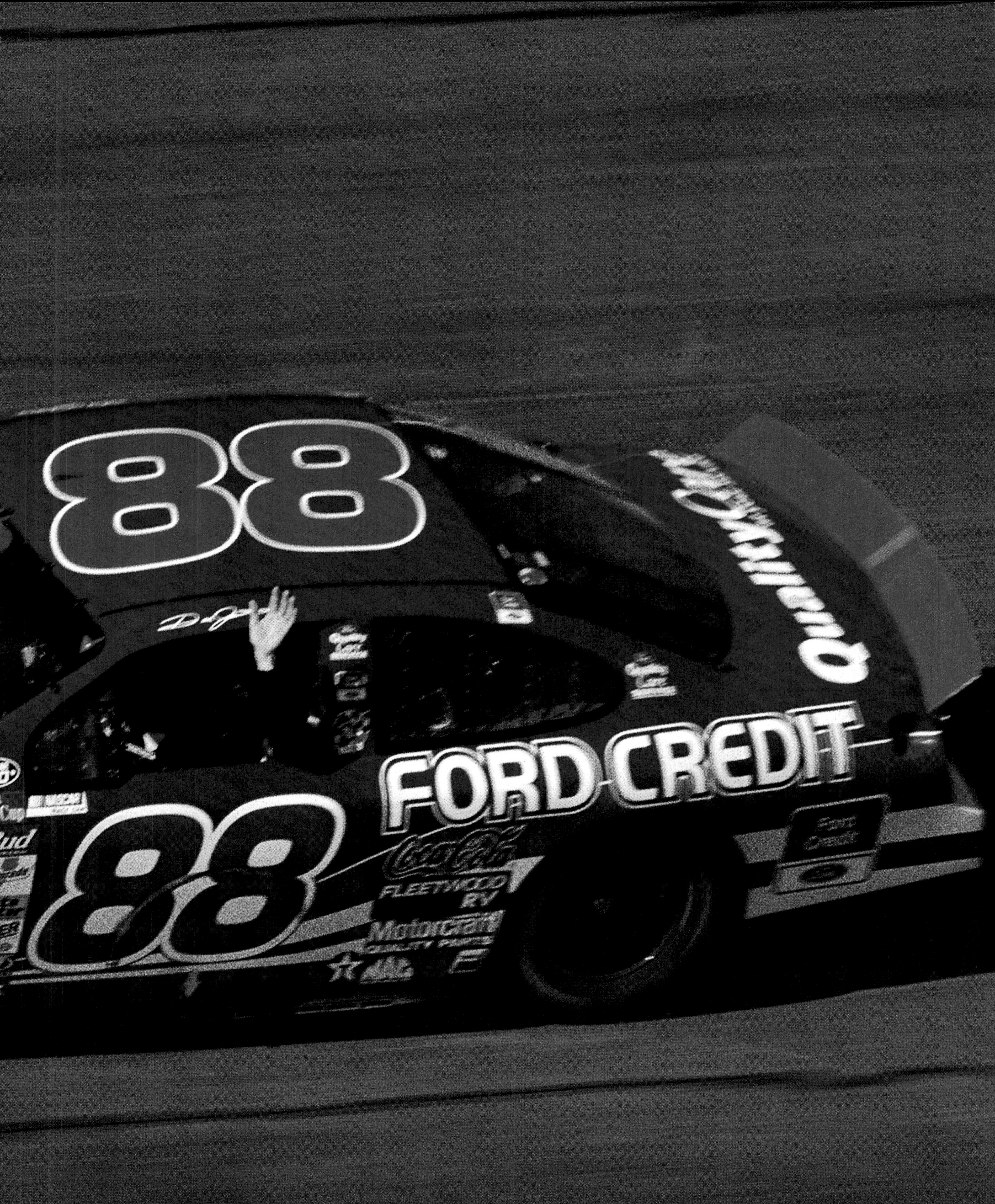
88
88
FORD CREDIT
FLEETWOOD
RV
Motorcraft

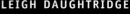

DAVE BLACK

ROBIN BOWMAN

MATTHEW NAYTHONS, M.D.

DAN HELMS

Robin Bowman is a New York–based freelance photojournalist and documentary photographer. Her photographs have appeared regularly worldwide in such publications as *Life, Le Figaro, Travel & Holiday, Forbes, Time* and *Stern*. Over the last few years, she has widened her scope, working on magazine and book projects that have taken her to Mexico, Finland, Haiti, Bosnia, Nepal, Israel and Cuba. And for the last several years her work has been chosen to appear in *Communication Arts Photography Annual*.

Matthew Naythons, M.D., juggled a career as an emergency room physician with world travel as an award-winning photojournalist for such publications as *Time, Newsweek*, and *National Geographic*, covering such stories as the fall of Saigon, the Jonestown massacre, and the Central American civil wars. In 1991 he founded Epicenter Communications in Sausalito, and continues to serve as the Chief Executive Officer and Publisher. Under his direction, Epicenter pioneered a series of user-friendly consumer guides to the world of new media as well as award-winning photojournalism book projects. In 1999, Dr. Naythons joined PlanetRx.com, an online pharmacy and health information website as Vice President of Editorial and Publisher.

Dave Black, a Colorado Springs–based photographer, is considered one of the leaders in the sports photography industry. His regular clients include *Newsweek*, Kodak, Coca-Cola,

Texaco, Reebok and *Sports Illustrated*. Dave has photographed world-class athletes and events for two decades, including each Summer and Winter Olympics since 1984. He's also a staff lecturer for the *Sports Illustrated* workshop and a featured speaker at various seminars and universities.

Leigh Daughtridge is a North Carolina native and a Chicago-based photojournalist. She attended the University of North Carolina at Chapel Hill, receiving her B.A. in journalism/mass communications in 1994. Leigh won the prestigious New York Festivals and International CINDY competition in 1997 for co-producing the multimedia documentary "Into Africa." Currently, Leigh works as central photographer for Copley Chicago Newspapers. Her work documenting Northern Illinois centenarians was recognized in this year's Pictures of the Year competition.

Dan Helms is a Miami-based photographer and a founder of the NewSport photo agency, which he manages. Dan's assignments have taken him worldwide and range from news to sporting events. He has covered the U.S. invasion of Panama, salmon fishing in Norway and the Olympics. His clients include *Newsweek, Sports Illustrated, National Geographic World*, Kodak, Coca-Cola, Chicken of the Sea and the U.S. Olympic Committee.